STOLEN
CHILDHOOD

Contemporary Issues of Family Breakdown

*A Report from the Lords and Commons
Family and Child Protection Group*

Co-editors

Revd. Lynda Rose and **Robert S. Harris**

Published by

Voice for Justice UK

First published in 2014 by Voice for Justice UK

PO Box 3837, Swindon SN3 9DS
E-mail: info@vfjuk.org

© Copyright The Lords and Commons Family and Child Protection Group

ISBN: 978-0-9929964-0-6

Cover Design and Typeset by TLB Direct, www.tlbdirect.co.uk

Printed in the UK by Interprint, Swindon, Wiltshire.
www.interprintswindon.co.uk

Commendation

The statement made by Jack Straw in the 1990s, "The family is the building block of society", has been quoted on many occasions, and yet family breakdown is a modern phenomenon from which flow many problems, particularly for our children.

I welcome the publication of this report, "Stolen Childhood", and commend its evaluation of some of the serious issues which we as a society are facing. The evidence provided in this report clearly demonstrates the defining value which stable families provide for our children.

Baroness Eaton DBE,
Chairman,
The Lords and Commons Family and Child Protection Group

Contents

Patricia Morgan is a writer and researcher, and the author of numerous books on family, crime and social policy, including *Family Matters: Family Breakdown and its Consequences* (a study in the New Zealand context); *Family Policies, Family Changes: Sweden, Italy and the UK* and *The War Between the State and the Family*. She was the author of *What Happens to Marriage and Families where the Law Recognises "Same Sex Marriage"?* This work was presented to the House of Commons Marriage (Same Sex Couples) Bill Committee, 1st March 2013. Her latest book, *The Marriage Files* was published in June 2014.

Chris Muwanguzi has worked with fathers in the UK since 2001, he initially worked with young fathers as part of the award winning Coram boysMEN project leading a team that developed innovative and ground breaking ways to engage with socially excluded young men, and fathers. Chris also worked as a consultant supporting a number of local authorities in inner and outer London to set up innovative ways to engage with fathers. He has also advised the UK government whilst serving on various panels regarding children and fatherhood. He is currently the CEO of the Family Matters Institute a national charity that:

- Provides **training** to the children and family workforce,
- Carries out **research** on family and relationships, and
- Develops interactive and innovative ways to engage with the public through **digital media.**

FMI also runs the largest fatherhood website in the UK – www.dad.info

Dr Josephine-Joy Wright currently works as the Lead for psychological services in CAMHS, 2gether Foundation Trust (Herefordshire). She is a Chartered Consultant Clinical Psychologist, specialising in Children and Family work, and complex adult neuro-developmental disorders, attachment, abuse and trauma. Since 1989 she has worked extensively with international disasters, including war-zones, pioneering psycho-social interventions, and developing work with child soldiers. She has also run and supervised Police Staff Support and Counselling Services, and trains teams and individuals in effective relationships, as well as undertaking specialist assessments and therapy with children and adults with neuro-developmental and attachment disorders, and traumatic/ abusive life experiences.

Dr Clifford Hill and Mrs Monica Hill have been involved in community work in inner-city areas of London for most of their married life. They both have an academic background of lecturing in social science and they jointly founded the Newham Community Renewal Programme. They have published more than 40 books and for the past 20 years they have been involved in the Lords and Commons Family and Child Protection Group and been responsible for publishing its research reports.

Preface

By Dr Clifford Hill and Mrs Monica Hill
Joint Conveners: Lords and Commons Family and Child Protection Group, July 2014

"The family is the building block of society," so said Jack Straw MP when, as Home Secretary, he was responding to the report "Family Matters" presented by the Lords and Commons Family and Child Protection Group in July 1998. The meeting was in the Moses Room in the House of Lords because at that time the Group was under the chairmanship of Lord Ashbourne.

The 1998 Report

Jack Straw went on to say that the health of society depended upon the health and stability of family life. He commended the quality of the research in the report and said that its conclusions and recommendations would provide a guide for the forthcoming White Paper on The Family, which he intended to introduce. The first three recommendations in the 1998 report were:

- The outstanding conclusion from the research we have studied shows that millions of children in Britain are suffering from the conflicts of their parents. As a nation we need to listen to their cries and give high priority to their needs.
- The research shows the lasting benefit to children of having their mother as a primary carer for the first six months of life and ideally until they are three years old. It also shows possible damage to children who are insecurely attached in infancy. Government policy should take note of these findings.
- It is recommended that the Government seeks to establish and implement a comprehensive policy involving both statutory and voluntary institutions to support and strengthen committed couple family life with marriage as the ideal.

The report urged a careful review of the work of the Child Support Agency in view of many complaints of injustice and unfair practice with particular discrimination against fathers. It went farther in stating:

- Britain is becoming a matriarchal society in which many men have lost their social role. Government needs to give urgent attention to tackling unemployment among young men to enable them to be role models for their children within the family.

The report noted that absent fathers played a large part in dysfunctional family life. It stated, "By the age of seven, 90% of children with committed fathers were in the household into which they were born, whereas only 27% of children of uncommitted fathers were still living with their natural parents."

Family Breakdown

It is more than 15 years since that report was presented in Parliament and was praised by the Home Secretary. Unfortunately, Jack Straw met considerable opposition within the Cabinet for his pro-marriage policies. He published a Green Paper but he was never able to present the White Paper which he promised, so the recommendations in the "Family Matters" report were never implemented. It would appear from the present woeful state of family life in Britain that successive Governments have either ignored the warnings and recommendations in the report, or have felt powerless to stem the tide of family breakdown.

In this present report "Stolen Childhood", the picture presented by Patricia Morgan, Chris Muwanguzi and Dr Jo Joy Wright shows the relentless increase in family breakdown that has taken place in the past three decades. It notes that the meltdown in marriage and stable two-parent families has resulted in more than 4 million children having their home life disrupted by the dissolution of their parents' relationship. Nearly half the nation's children are not living with their birth parents today by the age of 15. They are the innocent victims of the disputes and vagaries of their feckless parents.

But responsibility for the collapse of the traditional two-parent family in Britain does not only lie with a kind of social Darwinism whereby cultural norms have evolved from adherence to basic social values such as 'commitment', 'loyalty', 'integrity' and 'honesty', but it also lies with those responsible for political policy-making and with campaign lobby groups.

Fatherless Families

The situation in fatherless families is particularly acute and a matter for grave concern, not only because research shows that boys thrive far better with men at home, but also because this report highlights the social and psychological effects of family breakdown upon men that are all too often hidden from the public.

Men are expected in Western society to be macho and not to display their inner feelings, which often results in depressive, anxiety-related personality disorders which can lead to self-harm and suicide, if help is not available. There is a salutary warning in this that needs to be heeded and addressed.

Tributes

In presenting this present report to Members of Parliament in July 2014 the members of the Lords and Commons Family and Child Protection Group wish to pay tribute to those Members of the Commons and Lords who have supported the Group and materially contributed to its work.

We especially want to acknowledge Baroness Knight of Collingtree who, as Dame Jill Knight MP, founded the Group more than 20 years ago and presented its first report, "Violence, Pornography and the Media" to Members of both Houses in June 1996, with the support of Michael Alison MP, David Alton MP, and Donald Anderson MP. Sir Gerald Howarth MP chaired the Group for some 10 years, during which time three research reports were presented to both Houses. Two were on the subject of teenage pregnancy and underage sexual activity, while the third was a groundbreaking report on "The Cost of Family Breakdown" which is still quoted in both Houses today. More recently the Group has been chaired by Mr Jim Dobbin MP and the incoming chair is Baroness Eaton DBE. We warmly welcome her for the wealth of experience she brings to our work.

Introduction

By Revd Lynda Rose
CEO, Voice for Justice UK
Co-leader of the Sexualisation of Children Working Party, for the LCFCPG

'You've never had it so good!'

In the aftermath of World War II the nuclear family norm was a mother, father, and 2.5 children. With increased social mobility and growing affluence from economic stability, people may have mourned the demise of the extended family, but the bedrock foundations of society seemed solid, and generally speaking people were happy. Children grew up buttressed by the knowledge they had a place in the world – which by and large was still 'safe'. More than that, they knew that, whatever life might throw at them, they had the protection of a mother and father who would look after them - sometimes perhaps uncomfortably so - but glorying in their triumphs, comforting them in failure, and fighting for their success. At the end of the day, blood was thicker than water, and the family stood against the world! With some justification in 1957, Harold Macmillan assured us all, 'You've never had it so good!'

Fast forward to the 21st century, and that stable family norm has been all but obliterated – with devastating effect. Extraordinary as it seems, in the absence of armed global conflict, the hated symbol of both oppression and repression became… the family. So much so that in 1971 the Gay Liberation Front could state in the opening lines of their Manifesto that their goal was

…to rid society of the gender role system which is at the root of our oppression. This can only be achieved by the *abolition* of the family unit …Children must be liberated from the present condition of having their role in life defined by biological accident…[1]

Back in the day, these words would have been viewed by most ordinary citizens of planet earth as extremist claptrap, voiced more for effect than in hope of achievement, and therefore not really to be taken seriously. But the reality is that this was articulation of policy; and it is in process of achievement.

Irrespective of the issue of gay rights, the recent push for the legalisation of same sex marriage, as against already introduced provision for civil partnership, has radically undermined the status of this increasingly fragile institution, being yet another nail in the coffin of this once unassailable, stable and blood related unit. In our first article, 'Demographics of Disaster', Patricia Morgan clearly delineates the changing structure and erosion of family over the last half century, highlighting the devastating and demonstrable effect this has had on the nation's children. But, of course, it isn't just the children who have suffered, and one of the perhaps unforeseen by-products of liberation and the sexual revolution has been the detrimental effect on men. As the traditional family unit has fragmented, losing definition under pressure from the sequential relationships that form the new norm, the 'father' has become increasingly air-brushed from the lives of his biological children. This has undeniably harmed children, but it has injured men too, giving rise to grief at enforced separation, loss of identity and rights, coupled often with a sense of dislocation. Our second article by Chris Muwanguzi, of the Family Matters Institute, analysing the effects of modern family breakdown on both children and fathers, makes for uncomfortable and disturbing reading – but if we don't face the facts, we have no hope of providing a remedy.

However, while the socially fragmenting effects of increased family disintegration may be the subject of argument and date interpretation - which can be hotly contested

by both sides of the debate - one fact alone is irrefutable, and that is that young people today are increasingly suffering from mental illness, so much so that ever larger numbers are attempting – and often succeeding in – suicide. In the last section of this report, Dr Josephine-Joy Wright, a clinical psychologist with long experience of working with dysfunctional and abused children, shows how mental health problems amongst the young have reached an unprecedented high, one of the main reasons being the loss of personal identity and value that is direct result of family breakdown.

Stolen Childhood is a preliminary attempt to evaluate the problems flowing from the modern phenomenon of family breakdown. It will be followed in 2015 with a longer and more comprehensive analysis.

---

[1]   The opening of the Gay Liberation Front Manifesto 1971.

Demographics of Disaster?

By Patricia Morgan
Writer and Researcher

Research Findings

Married couples with children might still comprise the most common family household, but their numbers have been in long-term and increasing decline.

The light upturn in marriages in 2009 is likely to be due to a reduction in the number of residents of England and Wales marrying abroad. Otherwise, in 2010, there were 22 unmarried men and 20 women per 1,000 married, compared to 30.1 and 25.9 in 2000 and 42.1 and 36.1 in 1990. Unsurprisingly, the proportions who have ever married have declined in recent decades. Of those born in 1930, 90% of men and 94% of women had ever married by age 40 but, for those born in 1970, this was 63% and 71%. For those married by age 25, the figures are even starker: 51% and 74% of men and women respectively compared with 5% and 11% of men and women born in 1986 (the most recent birth cohort to reach age 25 in marriage data).

On present showing, the married population proportion is projected to fall to 42% by 2033. While, at the end of the first decade of the 21st century, married people in England and Wales numbered approximately 20.4 million (200,000 fewer than a decade before), cohabiters rose to nearly five and a half million (from four million a decade before) and single adults stood at 11m, having risen by three million over two decades. The proportion of non-married women aged 18 to 49 cohabiting increased from over one in ten (11%) in 1979 to more than one third (34%) in 2011.

Family Breakdown

By 2013, 24% of children were living with a lone parent in Britain and nearly a half of 15 year olds had experienced parental separation. This was partly the result of how around 34% of marriages end in divorce by their 20th anniversary (and 6% with death). Much is made of how the divorce rate has been decreasing since it peaked in 1988. Married couples' break-up rate may be falling, but this is decidedly not so for the rapidly growing proportion of unmarried couples.

If the 2006 British Social Attitudes survey found that two thirds of respondents thought there was 'little difference socially between being married and living together as a couple', they were sorely misinformed.[1]

Cohabiting couples make up 19% of couples with dependent children, yet account for 48% of family breakdown; being four to five times more likely to split up than married couples (or six times in a child's first five years). This is an average for couples with children under 16 of 1.3%. Selection factors (like age, education, income, and ethnicity) might explain part of consistently higher break-up rates amongst cohabiting parents, but cannot account for the doubling of family breakdown since 1980. Divorce rates may have stabilised over time, but nothing suggests that cohabitation has become more stable, rather the reverse.

As increasing family breakdown owes itself to the increasing proportion of cohabiting parents these are, in turn, related to the increase in births outside marriage which necessarily lead to increasing family breakdown and more lone parenthood.

In 2011, almost half of births in England and Wales were to unmarried mothers or a record 47.5% compared with 12% in 1980 and 6 per cent in 1960 and, as the size of married families contract, those of lone parents expand.

More couples have only one child compared with the two or more even a decade ago, while single mothers often have children in sequential relationships. There is evidence of an increase in the proportions of women having a child outside of any 'co-residential partnership' as much as within cohabitations.[2]

All this gives us an estimated 2.5 million of what are now called 'separated families' (although some may never have been together in the first place) with 4.1 million children. As 45% of 15 year olds are not living with both birth parents, a child born today may, on current trends, have less than a 50/50 chance of continually living with their original parents.

Cost of Family Breakdown

While it is hardly something that has happened over night, the meltdown in marriage and stable two-parent families has merited little or no concern at political and policy making levels and no remedial steps have been taken. Even the sheer monetary cost makes no impact. This is estimated at nearly £9 billion a year for lone parent benefits and maintenance payment collection. The State does little to recover the monies from absentee fathers, while supporting the mother when, should she live with the father, his contributions count against family entitlements. Add on all the extras for health, children in care, education, criminal justice, housing, and interventions for matters like domestic violence, and the Relationships Foundation think-tank estimates that family disintegration in the UK currently costs the public purse £46 billion a year - or £1,541 for every taxpayer.

Not only discriminated against in the tax/benefit system, but the married, two-parent family has been persistently condemned and routinely mocked. Demographic trends are often read to mean that this obsolete institution is deservedly on the way out – if not dead already – with commentators habitually highlighting its rarity or exaggerating its decline. These people often credit change with an authority of its own which we are all then expected to serve. Trends become a standard benchmark, meaning that the 'is' of what is happening in society, is treated as what 'ought' to happen, and must be welcomed and expedited. At the same time, disintegration is all a matter of happenstance, with the cumulative removal of legal, financial and other supports for marriage and married parents dismissed as no more than coincidental.

Diversity

At the same time, new 'family forms' are constantly being identified – akin to how 19th century anthropologists sought out lost tribes. Alternative 'families' include those 'living apart together' (LATs) – mostly under 25 and what would have once been described as boy and girl friends or courting couples.[3] The plurality ratcheted up to eclipse the conjugal family might be stages in the life cycle or where anyone happens to be at any point in time as when we are told how:

> There are more opportunities and more choices: marriage and re-marriage, cohabitation prior to or instead of marrying, lone parenting, non-heterosexual couples and families, young people and the elderly living alone. [4]

The diversity of family forms is anticipated to increase further - exemplified by 'blended families' or a shifting cast of presences in the home who effortlessly combine and separate as will and whim take them. It is presented as a "life course" which is:

> …full of exciting options. These include living in a commune, having a group marriage, being a single parent, or living together. Marriage is one life-style choice, but before choosing it, people weigh its costs and benefits against other options. Divorce is part of the normal family cycle and is neither deviant nor tragic. Rather, it can serve as a foundation for individual renewal and new beginnings. Marriage itself should not be regarded as a special privileged institution; on the contrary, it must catch up with the diverse, pluralistic society in which we live…[5]

Thus, while progressive elites imagine that marriage must "catch up" with the wonderful opportunities that are superseding it, these changes are nothing to worry about, let alone do they merit discouragement. Unlike divorce, splitting up and three or foursomes, the conjugal family is not only past its sell by date, but something we would best be rid of as soon as possible.

Even the welfare of children is used as a weapon against marriage, where any support would be a distraction from the prioritisation of youngsters' well-being. Instead, 'parenting' is meant to operate independently and irrespective of any 'family form' or adult relationship. An illustration of this approach is when the Minister of State for Children, Young People and Families (2005 to 2009), Beverly Hughes, declared that: "What children need is not marriage" but "love, stability, financial well-being and positive parenting." This oxymoron raises the question of how one is divisible from the other.

Already, the focal shift was marked by the Green Paper *Every Child Matters* (2003) and the Children Act 2004, or legislation to support the 'needs' of all youngsters with services provided by the state and in denial of any connection between adult relationships and their well-being.

The Case for Marriage

Yet, over four or more decades evidence has relentlessly piled up in favour of two parent families and marriage, not the reverse. This is a primary demonstration of how little or nothing in policy, at least in this area, owes to fact. The children of marriage have better outcomes in virtually every category of life compared to those reared by single, divorced or separated individuals, cohabiting couples, step parents, with foster families or in institutions.

A multitude of large scale, well conducted studies demonstrate how those born and raised in an intact marriage with two original parents are, on average, far more apt to avoid criminality and psychiatric problems: to truant less and achieve more educationally; become gainfully employed and, in turn, to successfully raise the next generation - after controlling for economic status and other factors.[6]

Parental marriage is associated with a much reduced risk of infant mortality and better physical as well as mental health, compared to other types of household arrangement. Girls raised outside marriage are far more likely to be young, unwed mothers, and boys to be delinquent, with lower education rates and high inactivity.[7] Such a family background increases the odds of children ending up in the lowest socio-economic stratum – by over 50% in some studies.[8]

Such findings are constantly repeated, are in one direction and have altered little, if at all, over time. For example, for 17,110 under 18s from the longitudinal National Health Interview Study, there was a 40% to 95% difference between children with both biological parents compared to those with previously or never-married mothers or in step families, when it came to school based problems like expulsion, suspension and behavioural referrals. For behavioural and emotional problems there is a threefold difference.[9]

Children's Outcomes

This applies across the world. Children who have been through family dissolution show similar rates for lower educational attainment, raised morbidity (overall 50% greater for boys) and reduced life expectancy to the UK and US.[10] It also applies in societies which have strived most to make lone parenthood fully functional.

Swedish boys with lone parents are five times more likely to die from drug or alcohol abuse and more than four times from violence. Girls are more than twice as likely to die by suicide, and three times more from drug or alcohol abuse. The risk of psychiatric disorder, suicide, suicide attempts and self-injury is more than double, and more than threefold for addictions. This is in the face of confident assertions that: "Swedish evidence suggests that if there is a difference between the children of lone mothers and those of couple-families with the same social and economic circumstances, it is that the former are more mature and self-sufficient."[11]

This might reflect the belief that developed welfare states, such as Sweden or Britain compared to the US, must make the role of parents less important, since money compensates for 'deprivation'. That family structure is as, or more, important in Sweden underlines its significance for upbringing – regardless, or in spite of, the largesse of welfare.

Risk Factors

While most adverse outcomes usually have roughly double or treble the prevalence among children not with original married parents, the exceptions are abuse and homelessness, where rates are vastly increased. A classic study found that pre-schoolers in step-parent homes had an estimated 40 fold risk of being abuse victims as same aged children with two natural parents.[12] All is at its worst in homes with 'multi-partnered fertility' where mothers have offspring in transient relationships with a sequence of uncommitted men.[13]

Deteriorating home circumstances are reflected in the rising care population and those considered to be 'at risk' (numbers on child-protection registers or the subject of protection plans in the UK increased to 50,552 by 2011 – from 32,492 in 2006). Most children who enter the care system come from lone parent homes, and a significant proportion of young prisoners, teenage parents, addicts and prostitutes come out of the care system.

There are indications of a substantial rise in psychosocial disorders - or conduct, hyperactive and emotional problems - affecting young people over the past 50 years.[14] The samples used are adolescent sweeps of the 1958 National Child Development Study, the 1970 Birth Cohort Study, and the 1999 British Child and Adolescent Mental Health Study. Conduct problems have shown a particularly strong rise and have long term implications - affecting socio-economic matters (benefit dependency, unemployment, homelessness, early parenthood etc), poor health and contact with the criminal justice system. It is estimated that two-thirds of NEET (not in employment, education or training) Job Seekers Allowance recipients aged 16 are from fragmented families.[15]

Absent Fathers

Children's immediate environment might, in turn, interact with factors like the greater availability of drugs, involvement in early sexual relations and deviant gang cultures which generate feedback loops that increase exposure to all manner of risks. Fatherless girls not only tend to fare poorly academically[16] but to mature and reproduce earlier. This is related to how father absence is often indicative of a stressed or highly conflicted childhood environment. Particularly when combined with the presence

of unrelated men in the home, this can mean very early sexual development and experience, often coerced.[17] Father absence is also associated with how boys with absent fathers are more likely to have had at least one child by their early 20s.[18] Along with early sex and motherhood for girls goes the Young Male Syndrome of father-free boys, where aggressive, risk-taking males have sex with as many females as possible. Gangs offer the immediate social comfort and protection that families, schools or welfare departments cannot provide.[19]

Boys thrive far better with men at home; something testified to by the tribulations of fatherless boys. Involved fathering helps to protect against depression or suicidality (thoughts and attempts); imparts views of what is right and wrong; encourages boys to consider being a father themselves and appreciate how both parents have responsibilities and deserve respect. In one of the more accessible studies, those labelled Can-do boys reported Highly Involved Men in their lives (91%) compared with only 9% in the Low Can-do group. In contrast, 72% of those with Dad Deficit were Low Can-do boys.[20] A quarter of boys with involved fathers had one or more problems, such as an anti-school ethos, depression and trouble with the police. None had all three, compared to more than one in ten of the Dad Deficit boys, where two-thirds had one or more problems. Dad Deficit is reinforced by a lack of constructive compensatory male models to show boys 'ways' of being a man. A spell in jail might be the first time a boy spends with adult males.

Criminality

As well as leaving more children with inadequate supervision, compromised security, fewer adult role models, and less inter-generational relationships, societies in which fathers are peripheral pose daunting problems of cohesion and control.

Those deprived of their role as providers and protectors may become predators themselves. Marriage is the variable with the strongest influence on male crime rates and the prospect of future law breaking. The longest study of crime in the world - based on the lives of 500 criminals who were in reformatories in 1930s/40s - identified three factors which lead men into law-abiding life – a steady job, a spell in the armed forces, and marriage.[21]

Marriage reduced re-offending by 40%, after controls for a multitude of other factors. In contrast, cohabitation reinforces or increases criminality.[22] Spouses make demands of each other and are more likely to work their way through adversities. Cohabitees stay in a relationship so long as they are happy and not overly controlled. The drastic drop in marriage for young men in recent times may account for much of the modern persistence in criminality as men age, when previously they would have withdrawn from such activities as they got older.

By embodying a set of norms, responsibilities and binding obligations, marriage not only encourages personal responsibility and altruism, but connects men to the larger community. Otherwise, male disengagement from family and work are primary causes for the disintegration of neighbourhoods.

Marriage and employment are often coterminous for men, particularly low or semi-skilled men. Economic responsibilities for family members provide the impetus to seek work, keep work, work longer and earn more. Marriage may mark a greater willingness to invest in human capital and, with performance crucial for outcomes, this translates into higher productivity, higher wages and faster wage growth.

Work is validated through responsibilities towards others – obligations that can enrich even the most menial tasks. The employment and wage gap by marital status has generational and ethnic aspects, where high workless rates and poor pay are related to various groups' levels of family commitments.[23]

It would be better for men, public safety, public finances and mothers and children if there were more live-in, working, married fathers. This may be the best bargain society can have, but it is at the heart of so much of the antipathy directed at the conjugal family – as when Nick Clegg chose the breadwinner husband as his symbol of oppression.

Abuse

A similar body of research for children demonstrates the advantages of marriage for adults with large nationally representative, longitudinal studies. All show benefits in terms of lower mortality rates, compared to the single, separated or divorced, with better physical and mental health, less addiction and exposure to violence.[24] This applies to all ages and both sexes, even if there may be a greater effect for men, seen most especially in mid-life, where the difference approaches threefold.[25] It is seen throughout the economic and ethnic spectrum.

Despite all the propaganda over the years that marriage is a licence for abuse, married women's victimisation rates are far lower than those of cohabiting or single women.

Boyfriends and cohabiters may be more violent than husbands because they have less to lose or invested in the relationship. Uncertainty over paternity may be an aggravating factor in the excessively high levels of violence experienced by unwed pregnant women which is seen throughout the economic and ethnic spectrum.[26]

Health

Controlling for personality and health risk behaviours reduces but does not eliminate the impact of marital status on health.[27] A meta-analysis examining 641 risk estimates from 95 publications, providing data on more than 500 million people, showed how this has been both modestly increasing over time and more rapidly for women.[28] Divorce and separation may have negative health consequences because, not least, fear, hostility and disturbance may affect cardiovascular activity and the immune system.[29]

People who live alone are particularly prone to excessive drinking, smoking and drug use, but non-smoking, non-alcoholic divorced men still have twice the mortality rate of married men.[30] Even after taking personality and risky behaviour into account, marital status affects survival into old age.[31]

Not only does single living or being unmarried increase serious risks to health, but the prognosis worsens for both sexes, regardless of age and treatment. [32] Men and women separated at the time of cancer diagnosis have the lowest survival rate, followed by the widowed and never married.[33] Marriage is associated with shorter hospital stays and fewer visits, as well as reduced nursing home admission.

It is argued that part of the advantage is attributable to selection: healthy, well-adjusted people are more attractive prospects and may be better able to cope with problems and sustain relationships. It is only part of the explanation, and marriage's health benefits are significantly reduced the second and third times around.[34] Again, despite Sweden's reputation as a welfare and equality pioneer, their lone mothers' health is as bad as Britain's - with rates of limiting long-standing illnesses between 50% and 60% higher than those for 'couple' mothers, who have the lowest deaths from suicide, assault, homicide or alcohol- related causes.[35] The less than good health of poor lone mothers increases over time and declines for poor couple mothers.[36]

Since married mothers everywhere have lower rates of depression compared to the single or cohabiting, this has implications for child welfare.

Suicide

The UK suicide rate has significantly increased in recent years. There were 4,552 male suicides in 2011 (18.2 per 100,000 population) and 1,493 female suicides (5.6 per 100,000). Patterns by marital status tracked over time show rates among married people to be consistently lower than for unmarried people of both sexes and all age groups. For single, divorced and widowed men aged 25 and over, these were three to four times higher than for married men between 1983 and 2004.

For single women, the differentials have increased to about threefold even if, for the widowed, these are fairly constant at about two and a half times higher. Similarly, 25% of divorced men have at some point had suicidal thoughts, compared with 9% for married men;

and two per cent of married men ever attempt suicide, compared with 9% of divorced men. Among divorced women, 28% and 11% respectively ever had suicidal thoughts or made a suicide attempt, compared with 13% and three per cent for married women.[37]

Unsurprisingly, increases in divorce and declines in marriage are the demographics most consistently associated with rises in suicide.[38] Danish studies have looked at time trends over a century (1906-2006); the longest period studied to date.[39] A one percent increase in divorce increased suicides by 0.52% and 1.12% for males and females respectively: a one percent increase in marriages reduced suicide by 0.77% and 0.63%. When factors such as employment status, income, ethnicity, psychiatric history and the clinical history of relatives are included, being unmarried is still a risk factor for both sexes.[40]

Other work using European cross-national comparisons and follow-ups (covering a multitude of people aged 30 plus, and 25,476 suicides in Austria, Belgium, Denmark, Finland, Turin, Madrid, Norway and Switzerland) found that while non-married, lower educational groups had a greater increased risk compared to the highly educated, marriage still had a generally protective effect for those more exposed to economic vicissitudes and stresses.[41]

Stronger welfare policies lacked any buffering effect, although involvement in public religious practices is associated with lower levels of suicidality (ideas and attempts) through the high levels of social support provided by religious communities.[42] This is paralleled by a time-series analysis using available suicide, social, economic and health data which focused on two age groups for whom trends have diverged in England and

Wales, or 25–34 and 60+ year olds.[43] Having a child lowers female risk – signalling the importance of attachment and responsibility for others.[44] Expectations that the differential suicide levels of the married and single must have reduced in recent years given the big increase in cohabiting are unmet.

Psychiatric Problems

Most people (estimates of 70-90%) who die by suicide have psychiatric problems - depressive, substance related, anxiety, psychosis, and personality disorders - with comorbidity common and self-harm a major risk factor. However, personal afflictions do not negate how suicide is more likely during times of strain or crisis, particularly if this undercuts social support. This is, again, party to ways that relationships have a positive affect through practical and emotional help and the control of risky or personally harmful behaviour.

As suicides for men in the 30-44 age group (23.5 deaths per 100,000) have recently overtaken those for younger men, there may be a 'cohort effect', as this particular generation has been most exposed to significant social changes, like the decline of traditional male jobs and lifelong marriages.

Unemployed and lower skilled men are ten times more likely to kill themselves than affluent men. It is here that unwed births, rising divorce and cohabitation, lone parent households, solo living and 'partnering and de-partnering', with all their stresses and lack of established status or position, are concentrated as manifestations of declining levels of social integration and recognition.[45]

There is a failure in Western societies to provide appropriate sources of social identity and attachment for (particularly lower status) males along with tendencies promoting unrealistic expectations of freedom and autonomy. This has left us with little short of a crisis in young male development with few growth points.[46]

Benefits of Marriage

At the most beneficial end of a sliding scale of relationships, marriage focuses social support and constraints in the intimate environment, not least because commitment profoundly alters how people deal with each other. The uncommitted are less likely to accept another's control, or change their behaviour at another's expectations or request, when no public promise has been made. Important for matters ranging from employment to alcoholism to criminality, it also diminishes mutual care and support.

Although cohabitation has rapidly become an alternative to marriage, it is less advantageous in all dimensions of mental and physical health. Conditional and provisional, with no forward trajectory, this may be entered precisely so that the participants can keep a foot out of the door, and be prepared to opt out if times get tough or other opportunities come along.

The effects of family structure continue to emerge, despite such a substantial body of evidence being routinely ignored, and despite the unfriendly or hostile treatment of marriage from publically funded university, charitable and other research organisations. It is incredible, considering marriage's erosion, and the opposition and disbelief it has faced, how marriage's advantages – personal health, longer lives, safer communities and better children – have endured at all.

All the demographic data cited in this article, unless otherwise stated, is available from the Office of National Statistics.

References

[1] Beaujouan, E and Bhrolcháin, M. N, Cohabitation and marriage in Britain since the 1970s, *Population Trends* 2011, 145.

[2] Kiernan, K, Cohabitation and divorce across nations and generations. CASE paper No. 65 2003, London School of Economics. http://sticerd.lse.ac.uk/Case and McLanahan, S, et al, Unwed Parents or Fragile Families? Implications for Welfare and Child Support Policy. 2001 In L.Wu and B. Wolfe (eds.), *Out of Wedlock: Causes and Consequences of Nonmarital Fertility*. Russell Sage Foundation: New York.

[3] Haskey, J, Living arrangements in contemporary Britain: having a partner who usually lives elsewhere and living apart together. *Population Trends* 2005, 122,35-45.

[4] Wertheimer, A & McRae, S, Family and Household Change in Britain. Research Results, Oct 1999, Economic and Social Research Council.

[5] Wilson, J.Q in Whelan, R (ed), *Just a Piece of Paper? Divorce Reform and the Undermining of Marriage*. 1995, Institute of Economic Affairs. p.78.

6   For over-views: Chapple, S. & Richardson, D (2009). Doing Better for Children. OECD. Amato, P, Children of Divorce in the 1990s: An Update of the Amato and Keith (1991) Meta-Analysis, *Journal of Family Psychology* , 2000:15, 355-370.

7   Ermisch, J, Francesconi M, and Pavelin D. J, Childhood Parental Behaviour and Young People's Outcomes, Institute for Social and Economic Research, University of Essex, 2002; also *Journal of the Royal Statistical Society,* 167, part 1, 2004, 69–101.

8   Biblarz, T.J, and Raftery, A. E, The effects of family disruption on social mobility, *American Sociological Review*, 58, 1993, pp.97–109.

9   Dawson, D.A, Family Structure and Children's Health and Well Being: Data from the 1988 National Health Interview Survey on Child Health, *J. of Marriage and the Family,* 1991, vol. 53, pp.572 -584. Manning, W.D & Lamb, K.A, Adolescent Well-Being in Cohabiting, Married, and Single-Parent Families, *J. Marriage & Family*, 2003:56, 876- 890. See also Pryor J & Rodgers B, *Children in Changing Families: Life after Parental Separation,* 2001 Oxford: Blackwell Publishers.

10   Ringback Weitoft, G et al, Mortality, Severe Morbidity, and Injury in Children Living with Single Parents in Sweden: A Population Based Study. *Lancet,* vol. 361, 9354, 25.01.2003. Unicef, *A League Table of Child Maltreatment Deaths in Rich Nations,* 2003, Innocenti Report Card, Issue no.5. Timms, D.W.G, *Family Structure in Childhood and Mental Health in Adolescence,* Research report 32 of project Metropolitan. Stockholm, Sweden: Univ of Stockholm, department of Sociology, 1991, 74, 78. Stattin, H & Magnusson, D, Onset of Official Delinquency, *Brit J of Criminology*, 1995: 35. 417-49. Tucker, J.S et al., Parental Divorce: Effects on Individual Behaviour and Longevity, *Journal of personality and Social Psychology,* 1997:73. 381-9. Singh, G.K & Yu, S.M., US Childhood Mortality, 1950 through 1993: Trends and Socioeconomic Differentials, *American Journal of Public Health,* 1995: 85 (4). 505-12. Jonsson, J,O & Gahler, M Fanukt, Dissolution, Family Reconstitution and Children's Educational Careers: Recent Evidence from Sweden. *Demography* 1997: 34. 277-93.

11   Duncan, S & Edwards, R, *Lone Mothers, Paid Work and Gendered Moral Rationalities*, 1999, Basingstoke: Macmillan Press Ltd. p34.

12   Daly, M & Wilson, M, Discriminative Parental Solicitude: A Biological Perspective. *Journal of Marriage and Family,* May 1980: 46.

13   Putnam, F.W, Ten Year Research Update Review: Child Sexual Abuse, *Journal of the American Academy of Child and Adolescent Abuse,* 2003: 42. 269-278.

14   Collishaw, S et al, Time Trends in Adolescent Mental Health, *Journal of Child Psychology and Psychiatry,* 2004: 45 (8). 1350-1362.

15   Cost of Family Failure Index. Relationships Foundation, 2014.

16   Heard H. E, The family structure trajectory and adolescent school performance. *Journal of Family Issues,* 2007: 28. 319–354.

17   Cherlin, A.J, Parental Divorce in Childhood and Demographic Outcomes in Young Adulthood, *Demography,* 1995 32, pp. 299-318. Belsky, J, Steinberg, L & Draper, P, Childhood experience, interpersonal development, and reproductive strategy: an evolutionary theory of socialization, *Child Development,* 1991: 62. 647–670. Belsky, J. et al & The NICHD Early Child Care Research Network (2007b), Family rearing antecedents of pubertal timing, *Child Development,* 78:1302–21. Draper P. Harpending H. Father absence and reproductive strategy: an evolutionary perspective, *J. Anthropol. Res.*1982:38. 255–273. Bogaert A. F. *2005,* Age at puberty and father absence in a national probability sample. *J. Adoles,* 2005:28. 541–546. Moffitt T. E et al, Childhood experience and the onset of menarche: a rest of a sociobiological model. *Child Development,*1992: 63. 47–58. Mendle J et al., Associations between father absence and age of first sexual intercourse. *Child Development,* 2009: 80. 1463–1480. Nettle D, Coall D. A, Dickins T. E, Birth weight and paternal involvement predict early reproduction in British women: evidence from the National Child Development Study, *Am. J. Hum. Biol,* 2010: 22, 172–179. Coall D. A & Chisholm J. S, Evolutionary perspectives on pregnancy: maternal age at menarche and infant birth weight,. *Soc. Sci. Med,* 2003: 57. 1771–1781. Nettle D, Coall D. A, Dickins T. E, Early life conditions and age at first pregnancy in British women, *Proc. R. Soc,* 201. 278, 1721–1727. Ellis, B. J. & Essex, M. J, Family environments, adrenarche, and sexual maturation: A longitudinal test of a life history model, *Child Development,* 2007:78:1799–817. Ellis B. J & Garber J, Psychosocial antecedents of variation in girls' pubertal timing: Maternal depression, stepfather presence, and marital and family stress, *Child Development,* 2000: 71(2) 485-501. Del Giudice, M Sex, attachment, and the development of reproductive strategies, *Behavioral and Brain Scienc,e* 2009: 32. 1–67. Andersson-Ellström A, Forssman L & IMilsom I, Age of sexual debut related to life-style and reproductive health factors in a group of Swedish teenage girls, *Acta Obstetricia et Gynecologica Scandinavica,* 1996: 75(5), 484-489. Ellis, B. J, Timing of Pubertal Maturation in Girls: An Integrated Life History Approach, *Psychological Bulletin* 2004:130 (6). 920-58.

18   Sheppard, P & Sear, R, Father absence predicts age at sexual maturity and reproductive timing in British men, *Biol. Lett.* 2012: 8 (2) 237-240.

19   Sergeant, H, *Among the Hoods*, 2012, Faber.

20   Leading Lads, 1999, TOPMAN in association with Oxford University.

21   Laub J.H & Sampson R.J, *Shared Beginnings: Divergent Lives,* 2004, Harvard University Press.

22   Horney J, Roberts J & Hassell K.D, The social control function of intimate partners: Attachment or monitoring? 2000. Paper for American Society of Criminology, San Francisco. California.

23   Akerlof, G. A, Men without children, *Economic Journal,* 1998, 108 (447): 287–309. P. Kostiuk, and D. Follmann, Learning curves, personal characteristics, and job performance, *Journal of Labor Economics,* 5, 1987. 533–60. Loh, E. S, Productivity differences and the marriage wage premium for white males, *Journal of Human Resources,* 1996:31. 566–89. Berthoud, R, Young Caribbean Men and the Labour Market, 1999, Joseph Rowntree Foundation, London.

24   US Department of Health and Social Services, The Effects of Marriage on Health, 2007. Waite, L & Gallagher, M, The Case for Marriage.

25   Rendall, M. S et al, The Protective Effect of Marriage for Survival: A Review and Update, *Demography* 2011:2. 481-506.

26   Jackson, N. A, Observational experiences of intrapersonal conflict and teenage victimisation: A comparative study among spouses and cohabiters, *Journal of Family Violence* 1996:11.191-203. Sorenson S.B, Upchurch D.M & Shen H, Violence and injury in marital arguments: Risk patterns and gender differences, *American Journal of Public Health* 1996:86 (1). 35-40.

27   Strohschein L, McDonough P, Monette G, et al., Marital transitions and mental health: are there gender differences in the short-term effects of marital status change? *Soc Sci Med,* 2005:61, 2293–303. Kim H. K, McKenry M, The relationship between marriage and psychological well-being, *Journal of Family Issues* 2002;23. 885–911. Sogaard A. J, Kritz-Silverstein D, Wingard D L, Finnmark heart study: employment status and parenthood as predictors of psychological health in women, 20–49 years, *Int J Epidemiol* 1994:23, 82–90. Johnson N.J, Backlund E, Sorlie P.D, et al., Marital status and mortality: the national longitudinal mortality study, *Ann Epidemiol* 2000;10, 224–38. Johnson N.J, et al., Marital status and mortality: the national longitudinal mortality study, *Ann Epidemiol* 2000:10, 224–38. Kiecolt-Glaser J. K, Newton T. L, Marriage and health: his and hers, *Psychol Bul,* l2001:127. 472–503. Johnson D.R & Wu J, An empirical test of crisis, social selection and role explanations of the relationship between marital disruption and psychological distress: a pooled time-series analysis of four-wave panel data, *J Marriage and the Fam,* 2002;64, 211–24. Rendall M.S, The Protective Effect of Marriage for Survival: A Review and Update 2011:2, 481-506. See the overview of evidence in *Why Marriage Matters: Thirty conclusions from social sciences.* Institute for American Values and National Marriage Project, 2011, Univ of Virginia.

28   Roelfs, D.J et al., The Rising Relative Risk of Mortality for Singles: Meta-Analysis and Meta- Regression, *Am. J. Epidemiol* 2011: 174 (4). 379-389.

29   Robles T. F, Kiecolt-Glaser J. K, The physiology of marriage: pathways to health. *Physiol Behav,* 2003:79. 409–16. Vogel, J, Economic Problems. Living Conditions and Inequality, 1975- 1995. *Levnadsfor hallanden,* 1997 rapport no.91, Statistics Sweden.

30   Rsengren A, Wedel H & Wilhemsen L, Marital Status and Mortality in Middle-aged Swedish Men, *American Journal of Epidemiology,* 1989: 129. 54-64.

31   Siegler I.C & Brummett B, Consistency and Timing of Marital Transitions and Survival During Midlife: the Role of Personality and Health Risk Behaviors, *Annals of Behavioral Medicine* 2013 45.

32   Lammintausta, A et al., Prognosis of acute coronary events is worse in patients living alone: the FINAMI myocardial infarction register. *European Journal of Preventive Cardiology,* Jan 30 2013.

33   Sprehn, G.C et al., Decreased cancer survival in individuals separated at time of diagnosis. *Cancer* 2009: 115. 5108–5116. Hughes M.E & Waite L.J, Marital Biography and Health at Mid-Life , *Journal of Health and Social Behavior,* 2009: 50. 344-358.

35   Gahler, M, Life After Divorce: Economical and Psychological Well-being among Swedish Adults and Children Following Family Dissolution. Dissertation series 32 (thesis), 1998, Stockholm: Swedish Institute for Social Research. Bjornberg, U Sweden: Supported Workers who Mother, in Duncan, S and Edwards, R, *Single Mothers in an International Context: Mothers or Workers?* 1997, London: UCL press. Weitoft G.R, Hagland B & Rosen M, Mortality among Lone Mothers in Sweden: A Population Study, *Lancet,* 2000: 355 8th April. 1215-219.

    Whitehead, M et al., Social Policies and the Pathways to Inequalities in Health: A Comparative Analysis of Lone Mothers in Britain and Sweden, *Social Science and Medicine,* 2000:50 255-70. Burstrom B et al., Lone Mothers in Sweden: Trends in Health and Socio-economic Circumstances, 1979-1995 *J Epidemiol Community Health,* 1999, 53 pgs. 150-56.

37   Meltzer H, Lader D, Corbin T, et al., Non-fatal suicide behaviour among adults aged 16–74 in Great Britain, 2002, The Stationery Office: London.

38   Gunnell D, et al., Why are suicide rates rising in young men but falling in the elderly? - a time-series analysis of trends in England and Wales 1950–1998, *Social Science & Medicine,* 2003: 57(4) 595-611.

    Agerbo E, Stack S & Petersen L, S, Social integration and suicide: Denmark, 1906–2006, *The Social Science Journal,* 2011: 48 (4) 630-640.

    Qin P, Agerbo E, & Mortensen P. B, Suicide risk in relation to socioeconomic, demographic, psychiatric, and familial factors: a national register-based study of all suicides in Denmark, 1981–1997, *American Journal of Psychiatry,* 2003: 160, 765–722.

41   Lorant, V et al., A European comparative study of marital status and socio-economic inequalities in suicide, *Social Science & Medicine*, 2005: 60 (11) 2431-2441. Agerbo E, Qin P & Mortensen P.O, Psychiatric illness, socioeconomic status, and marital status in people committing suicide: a matched case-sibling-control study, *Epidemiol Community Health* 2006: 60. 776-781.

    Robins A & Fiske A, Explaining the Relation between Religiousness and Reduced Suicidal Behavior: Social Support Rather Than Specific Beliefs, *Suicide and Life-Threatening Behavior,* 2009: 39 (4) 386–395.

43   Gunnell, D et al., Why are suicide rates rising ... *Op cit*

44   Qin P, Agerbo E, Mortensen P. B, Suicide risk in relation to ... *Op cit.*

    Rojas Y, Stenberg S, Early life circumstances and male suicide – A 30-year follow-up of a Stockholm cohort born in 1953, *Social Science & Medicine,* 2010: 70 (3), 420-427. Hawton K, Houston K & Shepperd R, Suicide in young people. Study of 174 cases, aged under 25 years, based on coroners' and medical records. *British Journal of Psychiatry* 1999, 175: 271-276.

46   Eckersley R & Dear K, Cultural correlates of youth suicide, *Social Science & Medicine,* 2002: 55 (11). 1891-1904.

The Impact of Family Breakdown

The Fathers' Voice: A research review and case studies into the impact of family breakdown on fathers and their families.

By Chris Muwanguzi
CEO Family Matters Institute

Case study 1

Thomas was a popular boy at school, he made friends easily and was helpful in class, he was really good at most of his subjects and only ever struggled with a couple of long and difficult words when he was reading. Thomas however has struggled with more than just a long and difficult word since his mother and father split up. He is often angry and gets into fights at school; he no longer likes to participate in activities and is no longer helpful. He is no longer the bright and promising pupil, and has now become the disruptive, challenging child at risk of exclusion.

This is a case study from Family Matters Institute SMILE programme but it is also the story of more than 100,000 under 16 year old children in the UK today, likely to experience the detrimental impact of family breakdown.[1]

Many children are able to survive the adverse impact of family breakdown[2], and where charities like ours, and many of our partners, are working with families to make sure that parents try to maintain a collaborative relationship and put their children first, our experience has been that there is a likelihood that the potentially long lasting impact for many of these children in some cases is not averted.

In the UK, one in three children will see their parents separate before they turn 18. (This includes breakdown of cohabiting relationships as well as divorce). Family breakdown has been estimated to cost the taxpayer almost £46 Billion in 2013, through effects on health, extra housing support, lost work hours, legal aid, and other related factors.[3]

Approximately one half of couples divorcing in 2010 had at least one child aged under 16, and over a fifth of those children were under five. Moreover, the number of children affected by divorce has risen over the past few decades, from approximately 82,000 (under 16 years) in 1971 to 100,000 in 2009.

What is often not considered is the wider impact on the family, particularly the impact on parents. Whereas children and mothers have traditionally been the focus of research on well-being after divorce, very limited attention has been paid to the fathers following divorce (Stone, 2001).

Professor Ridwan Shabsigh, of Cornell University in the U.S. and president of the International Society of Men's Health, said: 'Popular perception, and many cultures as well as the media, present men as tough, resilient, and less vulnerable to psychological trauma than women.' The fact is men get affected substantially by psychological trauma and negative life events, such as divorce, bankruptcy, war and bereavement.

Separation increases the risk of early death, substance abuse, suicide and depression. Divorced or separated men have a 39 per cent higher suicide rate than their married counterparts.[4] They are also more likely to take part in risky activities which increases their chance of early death.[5]

Case study 2

A case study by Dr Daniel Felix, of the University of Nebraska, centred on a 45-year-old white man who 'endured a difficult divorce'. He visited his family doctor for the first time in ten years, complaining of bad sleep and persistent abdominal pain. The man revealed he drank 'about a six-pack of beer a day,' had recently begun hating his job in middle management at a local bank and had become irritated with his colleagues and boss. He eventually reported having limited access to his children and paying a 'significant amount of child support'. The man also said his ex-wife, 'took all our friends with her after the divorce'.

The researchers reported the man's physical condition as 'unremarkable', apart from having a slightly enlarged liver and being somewhat overweight. They instead attributed his mild physical ailments and seemingly mild depressive state to continued anxiety and stress associated with his divorce.

So why the fuss about fathers? Why and how are they important to their children, and their partners?

To understand the extensive impact of family breakdown, it's best to start with the reason

children and families need their fathers.

Children really do benefit from having two parents fully involved in their lives, and usually want to retain as much contact as possible with their non-resident parent after separation. Most children hate the loss of contact with their fathers and often experience substantial distress, anger or self-doubt as a result.[6]

The impact of father relationship on child outcomes

1. Fathers influence their children in large part through the quality of their relationship with the mother of their children. A father who has a good relationship with the mother of their children is more likely to be involved and to spend time with their children, and to have children who are psychologically and emotionally healthier. Similarly, a mother who feels affirmed by her children's father and who enjoys the benefits of a happy relationship is more likely to be a better mother. Indeed, the quality of the relationship affects the parenting behaviour of both parents. They are more responsive, affectionate, and confident with their infants; more self-controlled in dealing with defiant toddlers; and better confidants for teenagers seeking advice and emotional support.[7]

2. Children with involved, caring fathers have better educational outcomes. A number of studies suggest that fathers who are involved, nurturing, and playful with their infants, have children with better linguistic and cognitive capacities.[8] Toddlers with

involved fathers go on to start school with higher levels of academic readiness.[9] They are more patient and can handle the stresses and frustrations associated with schooling more readily than children with less involved fathers. The influence of a father's involvement on academic achievement extends into adolescence and young adulthood. Numerous studies find that an active and nurturing style of fathering is associated with better verbal skills, intellectual functioning, and academic achievement among adolescents.[10]

3. Even from birth, children who have an involved father are more likely to be emotionally secure, be confident to explore their surroundings, and, as they grow older, have better social connections with peers. These children also are less likely to get in trouble at home, school, or in the neighborhood. Infants who receive high levels of affection from their fathers (e.g., babies whose fathers respond quickly to their cries and who play together) are more securely attached; that is, they can explore their environment comfortably when a parent is nearby and can readily accept comfort from their parent after a brief separation. A number of studies suggest they also are more sociable and popular with other children throughout early childhood.

The way fathers play with their children also has an important impact on a child's emotional and social development. Fathers spend a much higher percentage of their one-on-one interaction with infants and preschoolers in stimulating, playful

activity than do mothers. From these interactions, children learn how to regulate their feelings and behaviour. Rough and tumble with dad, for example, can teach children how to deal with aggressive impulses and physical contact without losing control of their emotions.

Generally speaking, fathers also tend to promote independence and an orientation to the outside world. Fathers often push achievement while mothers stress nurturing, both of which are important to healthy development. As a result, children who grow up with involved fathers are more comfortable exploring the world around them and more likely to exhibit self-control and pro-social behaviour.

Case study 3

A study of school-aged children found that children with good relationships with their fathers were less likely to experience depression, to exhibit disruptive behavior, or to lie, and were more likely to exhibit pro-social behaviour.[11] This same study found that boys with involved fathers had fewer school behaviour problems and that girls had stronger self-esteem. In addition, numerous studies have found that children who live with their fathers are more likely to have good physical and emotional health, to achieve academically, and to avoid drugs, violence, and delinquent behavior.[12]

4. Nurturing by a father serves several important purposes:
   - Fosters psychological well-being and self-worth in their children;
   - Helps fathers build close relationships with their children;

- Provides children with a healthy model of masculinity;
- Helps protect girls from prematurely seeking the romantic and sexual attention of men.

5. Another important function that fathers serve in the lives of their children is as guides to the world outside the home. When children are in preschool, fathers can best prepare their children for the outside world by engaging in vigorous, physical play and encouraging small steps in the direction of autonomy. For instance, fathers can push preschoolers to learn to dress themselves, to shake hands with house guests, and, more generally, to deal with the frustrations of daily life.

As children begin school, fathers can tell their children of their own experiences in school and encourage them to study hard, teach them about money management, or teach them a sport that will help their children learn about teamwork.

6. Certainly the role of father as protector and provider has changed over the years. Historically, fathers were viewed as chief financial provider for, and protector of, their children. As the traditional roles of mother and father, and likewise man and wife, have changed over the years, the distinctions have blurred, especially when it comes to who is the breadwinner.

One study, however, found that men view marriage, "as a partnership of equals, albeit one in which the man is the partner ultimately responsible for the provision of income and the family's protection".[13]

The ability to provide and protect is still, today, very much tied up with the average man's sense of self and sense of manhood. Research consistently shows that fathers who are employed full-time express more happiness with family life and have better relationships with their children, compared to fathers who are underemployed or unemployed.[14]

7. While the direct relationship a father has with his child is of paramount value, fathers also exercise a strong influence on their children through the type of life they live in and outside the home. Being a role model is an important task. In the way that fathers treat other people, spend their time and money, and handle the joys and stresses of life, they provide a template for living for their children that often proves critical in guiding the behavior of their children, for better or worse.

As discussed earlier, a father's treatment of the opposite sex, his ability to control his own emotions, and his approach to work, all play a formative role in shaping his sons' and daughters' approach to romantic relationships and marriage, interpersonal relationships, and school and work.

Research into the impact of divorce on fathers, and listening to the voices of the fathers that come to find help through Family Matters Institute's parenting website, DAD.info forum, has found -

1. That most fathers struggle emotionally during the process of, and after, divorce. This, for many men, is probably one of the biggest aspects of the whole catastrophe. The end of the marriage takes a sombre toll on most fathers' emotional state as most men tend to tie everything they have to their marriage. The results for most men are:

- Depressive disorder
- Anger
- Resentment
- Suicidal Thoughts
- Emasculation
- Isolation
- Worry and Panic

Taking it on the chin and just moving on, therefore, cannot be done so easily when you don't have your home, your children, and a lover or partner to be supportive of you. The foundation to their identity and life is completely broken, and the more they try to hide these mental pitfalls, the worse it becomes.

2. Many men find themselves in circumstances of being middle aged and feeling like they are struggling the way they once did when much younger, despite a better profession or enterprise. If they have job troubles, due to the separation and their emotional state, this can cause even greater impact post-divorce.

3. A man's sense of being a good father is often destroyed by divorce. Most fathers end up not having custody of their children and, if at all, have to settle for visiting them on the weekends. Our experience has been that for many men this has left a deep sense of unworthiness, combined with emotional and social hurt caused by the almost automatic assumption the relationship breakdown was their fault, and that they are therefore unable to care for their children.

4. Fathers experience a loss of character and identity. To be separated after investing so much effort into building a home and marriage, coupled with the sense of identity as 'husband' and maybe 'father', is devastating. The finality of separation brings with it, for the man, realisation that he is no longer the person he thought he was.

On Dad.info, most men have reported in their posts, and in peer to peer conversation, that they have been left less angry and resentful of their partner, but struggle more with:

a. Isolation from their children, their wider families and friends – having to establish new connections;
b. Parental alienation;
c. Struggle to maintain productivity at work;
d. Financial pressures – including child support, financing a new home, often having to pay for the old one too;
e. Missing the everyday world of seeing their children growing up;
f. Very little access to their children, as well as stressful court proceedings.

Children of separated families have a higher probability of:

- Being in poverty and poor housing;
- Being poorer when they are adults;
- Behavioural problems;
- Performing less well in school;
- Needing medical treatment;
- Leaving school/home when young;
- Becoming sexually active, pregnant, or a parent at an early age;
- Depressive symptoms, high levels of smoking and drinking, and drug use during adolescence and adulthood.

Factors affecting outcomes:

- Financial hardship can limit educational achievement;
- Family conflict before, during, and after, separation can contribute to behavioural problems;
- Parental ability to recover from distress of separation affects children's ability to adjust;
- Multiple changes in family structure increase the probability of poor outcomes;
- Quality contact with the non-resident parent can improve outcomes;
- Divorce might leave some with a broken heart, but it also causes real health problems for men, according to researchers;
- Those whose marriages end have higher rates of mortality, substance abuse and depression, and often lack social support, a study found. It called for doctors to refer more male divorcees to therapists and said more work is 'urgently needed' to investigate the damaging effects of relationship break-ups on their health;
- American researchers say that divorced and single men have a 39% higher suicide rate than their married counterparts - perhaps in part because they are more likely to engage in risky behaviour.

There is emerging evidence that high paternal involvement may be correlated with greater family stability:

- Low father involvement is associated with women's anger towards their partners.[15]

- High take-up of parental leave by Swedish fathers is linked to lower rates of separation/divorce, as is more equitable sharing by a couple of earning and caring roles. In fact, couples are 30% less likely to break up when the father has taken some parental leave – i.e. leave over and above the 10 days' leave most Swedish fathers take when their babies are born.[16]
- An important longitudinal study which controlled for socioeconomic factors found fathers' involvement in routine, every day childcare, plus play/school liaison throughout a child's life to beyond adolescence, accounting for 21% of the variance in fathers' marital happiness at midlife.[17]
- In Australia, it was found that men's involvement in infant care positively correlated with their satisfaction with family life and adjustment to fatherhood.[18]
- Among cohabiting couples with newborns, both parents' beliefs that father-involvement is important, plus fathers' actual involvement (measured here by regular nappy-changing), were found to predict relationship stability.[19]
- The importance of working with both partners on their beliefs and aspirations relating to parenting is clear: one study of new parents found that a couple relationship that was happy and appeared stable at the time of the birth, could be seriously and quite quickly eroded when partners held different ideas about parenting.[20]

References

1   ONS England & Wales, Layard & Dunn, 2009.
2   Neale & Flowerdew, 2007.
3   Relationships Foundation - http://www.relationshipsfoundation.org/Web/OnlineStore/Product.aspx?ID=154vCan%20March%202014
4   Journal of Men's Health. Authors Daniel Felix, W. David Robinson, and Kimberly Jarzynka. Sept 2011.
5   McCall, Patricia L, and Land, Kenneth C, Trends in White Male Adolescent, Young-Adult, and Elderly Suicide: Are There Common Underlying Structural Factors? *Social Science Research*, Vol. 23, pp. 57-81, 1994.
6   A good childhood: Searching for Values in a competitive age, by Richard Layard & Judy Dunn, 2009.
7   Cummings, E. M., & O'Reilly, A. W. 1997. Fathers and family context: Effects of marital quality on child adjustment. In M. E. Lamb (Ed.), The role of fathers in child development (3rd ed., pp. 49-65, 318-325). New York, NY: John Wiley & Sons; Lamb, M. E. (1997). Fathers and child development: An introductory overview and guide. In M. E. Lamb (Ed.), The role of fathers in child development (3rd ed., pp. 1-18, 309-313). New York, NY: John Wiley & Sons.
8   Erini Flouri, Department of Social Policy and Social Work, University of Oxford, The Role of Father involvement and mother involvement in adolescent psychological well-being. Sarah Allen PhD, Kerry Daly PhD, University of Guelf, The Effects of father involvement, 2007.
9   National Center for education statics, 1997, Flouri Buchanan & Bream, 2002, Flouri, 2005.
10 Pruett, K. 2000. Father-need. New York, NY: Broadway Books; Sternberg, K. J. (1997).
11 DFE's paper on review of best practice in parental engagement by Janet Goodall and John Varhaus.
12 The relationship between family structure and adolescent substance abuse., Rockville, MD: National Clearinghouse for Alcohol and Drug Information; Harper, C., & McLanahan, S. S. (1998). Father absence and youth incarceration. Paper presented at the Annual Meeting of the American Sociological Association, San Francisco, CA; Brenner, E. (1999). Fathers in prison: A review of the data. Philadelphia, PA: National Center on Fathers and Families.
13 UN Nations report, Men in Families and Family Policy in a Changing World, NY, 2011.
14 Weiss, R. S. Men and their wives' work. In F.J. Crosby (Ed.), Spouse, parent, worker: On gender and multiple roles. 1987.
15 Ross & Van Willigen, 1996.
16 Olah, 2001.
17 Snarey, 1993.
18 Lupton & Barclay, Australia, 1999.
19 Hohmann-Marriott, 2006.
20 Cowan & Cowan, 2000.

Mental Health In Britain's Young People:
Is Our Next Generation Choosing Death Or Life?

By Dr Josephine-Joy Wright

Clinical Psychologist, CAMHS, 2gether Foundation Trust (Herefordshire)

The Facts

In 1995, the Department of Health published "A handbook on child and adolescent mental health" which cited that, although 10-20% of young people required help for mental health problems at some point in their lives, severe mental illness was rare in young people. Only 7.6 per 100,000 15-19 year olds were seen to struggle with suicide, and bullying was not identified as a significant factor affecting children's mental health (except to be embraced in the general clause of "physical, sexual and emotional abuse").

Contrast this with the NSPCC's 2013 report that a third of Britain's young people experience suicidal thoughts and ideation. Peter Wanless, CEO of NSPCC in his work with ChildLine last year said:

> The issues facing children today are very different from those that faced us as children. Stranger danger, for example, rarely comes up in contacts to ChildLine but depression, self-harm, online bullying and even suicide contacts are increasing exponentially.

This statement echoes the National Children's Home assertion in 2002 that one in four children in Britain have been bullied by phone or internet, 6% in a threatening way, and that such bullying is a major risk factor in the development of Depressive and Anxiety-related disorders. In March 2013, the NSPCC stated on their website that 38% of young people said that they had experienced cyberbullying. Indeed, Marilyn Campbell (2005) termed cyberbullying and its impact on child and adolescent mental health as "an old problem in a new guise" and in Queensland, Australia's Commission for Children and Young People in June 2013 published research linking suicide to cyberbullying.

In the UK, a recent investigation led by Tanya Bryon provided preliminary support for such findings, and the British Medical Journal Open 2013 published The Health Improvement Network's survey of 479 GP practices, which showed that amongst 10-18 year olds, 81 had committed suicide, 1496 had attempted to do so and 1176 said that they had experienced suicidal ideation.

So what is happening to our young people? Are these figures new, or are we simply becoming more aware of the risk factors which affect young people's mental health, and giving the previously "silent generation" permission to speak about their pain and distress?

The Problems

In 1995, in the *Health of the Nations* report,

the interest in child and adolescent mental health was to reduce the distress to children and families, to reduce the incidence of adult mental health from untreated children's mental health problems, and to reduce the cost of mental health problems on services.

Today, the first of these factors is given greater prominence. We are berated for being sixteenth in the UNICEF table for child and adolescent emotional wellbeing, as against other rich nations, and Young Minds and NICE provide startling statistics that 72% of young people in care and 95% of young offenders have mental health problems, with double the incidence of childhood depression now compared with the 1980s. This reflects the incidence of mental health problems mentioned in the National Statistics (1999) survey of child and adolescent mental health (4% depression; 1 in 10 mental health problems), compared to recent findings by NICE and Young Minds.

The Association for Young People's Health Key Data (2013) confirms that suicide rates among young men have fallen since 2001, and in 2011 were 13.3 per 100,000, but this is not true of female suicides. Now, rather than 1 in 10, 13% of boys have mental health problems.

In my 30 years of clinical experience, now more than ever, young people speak of feeling isolated, struggling with family conflict and difficult breakdowns, and with emotionally absent parents leaving them alone to try to make sense of huge peer and media pressure to look, be and behave in certain ways.

Family Breakdown and the Cost to Children

Back in 2009, Mooney, Oliver and Smith undertook a review of the evidence into the "Impact of Family Breakdown on Children's Wellbeing". They showed that the key factors were not simply family breakdown, per se, but the way the breakdown was managed; the presence of violence, conflict, poverty, and poor parenting all contributing, as well as, in particular, parental mental health problems, which greatly exacerbated the incidence of poor mental health in children. With the increasing isolation of families and fragmented communities in the UK, these risk factors are even more pertinent.

Amato et al (1995) and Dunn et al (2004) have particularly detailed the importance of the quality of parental relationships, especially non-resident fathers. If fathers are close and involved in their lives, children are seen to have fewer adjustment problems and greater academic success. For both fathers and mothers, involvement, affection, support and limit setting were found to be crucial in affecting children's outcomes, especially adjustment and mental health.

"Think child, think parent, think family: a guide to parental mental health and child welfare", emphasised the impact of parental mental health on young people's own mental health, as well as the pressures on children having to act as carers. Lack of parental support and mentoring, combined with community isolation, all profoundly impact children's life experiences.

The Rise of Mental Health Problems

One in five adults experience mental health problems during their lifetime and, at the time of their illness, 1:4 will be parents. That leaves a significant number of children affected. Yet the support for such children is minimal. As parental support and good relationships between children and parents, and with school, are the most significant protective factor in preventing young people's mental health problems, no wonder many of these young people struggle, suffering in silence or themselves developing mental health problems.

With an escalating number of admissions to hospital for eating disorders, and high incidences of undiagnosed adolescent depression being the greatest predisposing factor for adolescent suicide, something is going wrong (half of all lifetime cases of psychiatric disorders start before the age of 14 years). The National Collaborating Centre for Mental Health, 2012, estimates 1:250 females and 1:2000 young males experience anorexia nervosa, with five times this number reporting bulimia nervosa. The NCCMH acknowledges that, as for self-harm, adolescent eating disorders are severely under-reported.

The same is certainly true for suicide attempts. The Centre for Suicide Research in Oxford found that in a sample of 174 under-25 year old suicides, unemployment, lack of family support, relationship difficulties and, vitally, undiagnosed and untreated depression (in 55.5%), were significant factors leading to the suicide.

We may be more economically wealthy, with greater opportunities for mobility and international travel and communication now than in previous decades, but somehow something is not working. We are failing our children and young people.

What can we do?

The Queensland report cited above also explored how to reduce young people's risk of suicide, and specifically targeted reducing cyberbullying. They found that parental involvement was crucial; strong parent-school links and parents who were involved in their children's lives, helping them to develop strong coping strategies, good relationship skills and helping them to say 'no' to abusive behaviours and recognise safe relationships.

Farrell and Barrett (2007) explored the risk and protective factors which affect the incidence of anxiety and depression in young people, and found that significant preventative protective factors are the parent-child relationship, and the level of attachment, monitoring and involvement of parents in young people's lives. Also of significance was the level of community involvement in the young person's life and good school-parent-home links. They discussed the evidence-based FRIENDS programme as an effective preventative factor, involving as it does sessions for schools, parents and young people to enhance their coping and their emotional literacy and resilience.

In the UK the focus is still on helping parents parent under-5s practically, such as feeding, washing and developmental milestones; yet parents are routinely given very little help with how to enhance children's ability to cope emotionally and manage effective relationships, which are crucial protective factors in young people's mental health. We need to fund long-term sustainable programmes to enhance parental involvement and parent- school cooperation.

Inter-agency co-operation

Across the reports cited above, the need for clear inter-agency working and continuity of care is a recurring theme. It constantly bemuses me why we designate children's services, especially Tier 2 and 3 **Child and**

Adolescent Mental Health Services
(CAMHS), as 0-18 years, when our educational provision is 0-19 and young people's eighteenth birthdays fall in their final A level year. In CAMHS we are meant to transfer vulnerable young people to adult care when their whole world is changing!

We need to commission and develop fully integrated mental and physical health, social care, police and education services for 0-19, or even up to 25 years, with all agencies working out of shared hubs of provision in the community. We need dedicated inter-agency services for 14-25 year olds to assist with the vulnerable transition into adulthood.

We need to challenge and equip parents to acknowledge the huge protective factor which they themselves play in their child's mental health. We need to encourage the development of evidence-based school and community policies and programmes of integrated parent-school liaison, such as FRIENDS, to raise awareness among parents, teachers, support workers and young people, and to enhance interest and involvement, and thus supervision of young people, by parents so they become secure bases where children can go with their worries and fears, thus reducing their vulnerability to abuse and bullying.

Government funding of superb organizations such as Papyrus, which campaigns to tackle the causes of young people's suicide, is vital. If we are genuinely to implement the 2013 Suicide Prevention Strategy and tackle the stain of young people's growing mental health problems on our nation, we need to promote further evidence-based research into the underlying factors, as well as being serious about our response as a nation.

Support networks for vulnerable young people

We need to work with young people to understand why and when they are vulnerable and provide them with networks of support. We need to use such findings to raise awareness among parents, teachers, and communities, as well as young people themselves, of mental health problems in young people, to reduce the incidence of undiagnosed, untreated depression and other mental health problems, thus reducing suicides. In a recent project with a group of young people in Hertfordshire we have developed an App (called "BAPPIE"), which seeks to assist this process.

We need to all take up the challenge to tackle and stamp out cyberbullying and internet and relationship abuse. Abuse is mucky, abuse wrecks lives. It is the responsibility of us all.

Similarly, it is our responsibility to be aware of the impact on children of our relationship difficulties. If we are to really guide and nurture children and young people, creating an emotionally healthy Britain, we as adults have to practice what we hope and dream for them in our own lives. If we embrace life, we show them the way to life.

I work every day in NHS and social/education services that are having to cut-back hard to become viable and cost effective. But this matter cannot wait. We cannot afford not to act now. Too many children and young people have died. Too many families are grieving or living in the hell of emotional distress. We have to all take responsibility for the mental health of the next generation. Then we will have a Britain in which they want to live.

References

Amato, PR, Loomis, LS and Booth, A. Parental divorce, marital conflict and offspring well-being during early adulthood, *Social Forces*, 73, 895-915, 1995.

Dunn, J, Cheng, H, O'Connor, T and Bridges, L. Children's perspectives on their relationships with non-resident fathers; influences, outcomes and implications, *Journal of Child psychology and Psychiatry*, 45 (3), 553-566, 2004.

Farrell, L and Barrett, P. Prevention of childhood emotional disorders: reducing the burden of suffering associated with anxiety and depression, *Child and Adolescent Mental Health*, vol. 12 (2), May 2007.

Hagell, A, Coleman, J and Brooks, F. Key Data on Adolescence, Association for Young people's Health, *Public Health*, England, 2013.

Meltzer, H and Gatward, R. The mental health of children and adolescents in Great Britain, Office for National Statistics, 1999.

Mooney, A, Oliver, C and Smith, M. Impact of Family breakdown on Children's Well-being: Evidence Review, Department for Children, Schools and Families; Thomas Coram Research Unit, Institute of Education, University of London, 2009.

Rushton, A and Dance, C. Quality protects: a commentary on the Governmental agenda and the evidence base, *Child and Adolescent Mental Health*, 7 (2), 2002.

Rutter, M, How the environment affects mental health, *British Journal of Psychiatry* special editorial, 2005.

A handbook on child and adolescent mental health, The Health of the Nation", DoH, 1995.

Emerging Findings. Getting the Right Start: The National Service Framework for Children, Young People and Maternity Services, DoH, 2003.

No Health Without Mental Health", DoH, 2011.

Preventing Suicide in England: A Cross-Government Outcomes Strategy to Save Lives, September, 2012.

Suicide in Young People, Centre for Suicide Research, Oxford, 2013.

Suicide remains the highest cause of death in young people, Papyrus press release, 2014.

Think child, think parent, think family: a guide to parental mental health and child welfare, Social Care Institute for Excellence, December 2011 (review 2014).

Conclusion

By Robert S. Harris
Co-leader of the Sexualisation of Children Working Party, for the LCFCPG
Director, Voice for Justice UK

Social commentators have, on occasion, asserted what they judge is the preeminent test by which any society can presume to be civilised. They suggest that it is not ultimately based on whether there is a developed infrastructure of roads and utilities, though these inevitably form a crucial part of any modern society. Rather, it is thought that the benchmark of a civilised society is measured according to how it treats its women, senior citizens, the disabled, the mentally ill, and its children. If a society is to fully appreciate its children, surely it must fully grasp the central role a strong family has for a child's upbringing?

In this report, the body of evidence cited demonstrates clearly the pivotal value a stable family bears upon the welfare and life prospects of children.

Patricia Morgan pointed out that by 2013, "24% of children were living with a lone parent in Britain and nearly a half of 15 year olds had experienced parental separation." To appreciate this in the wider context, it was highlighted that cohabiting couples constitute 19% of couples with dependent children, yet they account for 48% of family breakdown, "being four to five times more likely to split up than married couples (or six times in a child's first five years)."

These demographics highlight how crucial it is for children to be raised in a two-parent home, ideally where the parents are married. While children do indeed grow up in a variety of 'family forms', we should not feel coerced by political sensitivities, so that we marginalise the primary role of married parents in the lives of children. Can anything less be in the child's best interests?

Chris Muwanguzi makes a compelling case to show how significant fathers are in the development of children. He also demonstrates how a child's future life prospects are vitally influenced by their father's positive involvement in their upbringing. Such involvement bears directly on physical and mental health outcomes, as well as academic achievement.

All of this strongly points to the need for legislation and public policy to be more sensitive to, and accommodating of, the far-reaching role and contribution played by fathers in the lives of their children, than is true under the current system.

Compellingly, the shocking rise in mental illness amongst young people, clearly set out by Dr Josephine-Joy Wright, underpins the claims of her fellow contributors. Dr Wright points out that only a couple of decades ago there was a low incidence of mental illness amongst children. She puts the blame squarely on the unprecedented increase in family breakdown. Depression, self-harm, online bullying and suicide are all, she says, clear evidence of children's inability to cope with family conflict and absence of stability.

The family is famously and rightly described as 'the bedrock of society.' A phrase such as this, used repeatedly, risks slipping into the realm of cliché. So there is a real possibility that the full meaning of 'the bedrock of society', especially as it applies to the flourishing of children, is diminished. It is hoped this report will prompt legislators to consider further how best law and public policy can meaningfully promote families with married, opposite sex, parents. On the evidence, anything less does not enhance childhood, but robs it.